CONTENTS

Published By Century Books Limted,
Unit I, Upside Station Building,
Solsbro Road, Torquay, Devon, TQ2 6FD.
books@centurybooksltd.co.uk   Published 2011.

©2011 N-Dubz Music, LLP.
Under license to Bravado Merchandising.
All rights reserved.

www.ndubz.com

GETTING TO KNOW...
DAPPY

FULL NAME
Costas Dinos Contostavlos

NICKNAMES
Dappy, Dino

DATE OF BIRTH
11th June 1987

PLACE OF BIRTH
Camden Town, London

EYE COLOUR
Brown

FAVE FOOD
Proper Greek salad

THERE COULD ONLY BE ONE DAPPY BECAUSE...
He wows the fans with his crazy hats, he writes killer tunes and has bonkers, boundless energy.

DAPPY LOVES TO...
Write music, rap and go to theme parks

MOST LIKELY TO SAY...
"NaNaNiiiii!"

DID YOU KNOW?
Dappy and his girlfriend Kaye are proud mum and dad to two little boys called Gino and Milo.

STYLE FILE DAPPY

Dappy has been expressing himself through his style ever since he was a little kid! The rapper is never afraid to stand out from the crowd, blending urban street fashion with the latest sportswear. There is one essential accessory that defines the star's look more than anything else – his amazing collection of hats.

As well as cool clothes, Daps boasts some very personal works of body art. His first tattoo is on his right forearm – the names 'Dappy' and 'ND' decorated with bandana patterns. In tribute to his beloved dad Byron, he has 'RIP Dad' inked onto his neck. You might also have spotted the words '2LISA' on Dappy's left arm, in homage of course to his talented cuz.

Style certainly mean a lot to N-Dubz's main man. At the Royal Variety Performance in 2010, he even ended up talking fashion with His Royal Highness Prince Charles!

"I was star struck, but I felt kind of confident because I was wearing this sick suit made by Vivienne Westwood. Charles said, 'Where did you get that suit?' And I told him it was tailored precisely for my body by Vivienne."

Apparently the Prince was so impressed, he said he might have to order one for himself one day.

NaNaNiiiii!

GET THE LOOK

- Mix your fave sports labels with glitzy bling.

- Shake things up by teaming hats with hoods.

- Give plain gear some punch by layering on crucifixes, desert scarves and slogan tees.

- Get yourself a fierce new hairstyle or experiment with eyebrow stripes.

GETTING TO KNOW...
TULISA

FULL NAME
Tula Paulinea Contostavlos

NICKNAMES
Tulisa

DATE OF BIRTH
13th July 1988

PLACE OF BIRTH
Camden Town, London

EYE COLOUR
Blue

FAVE FOOD
Anything cooked up by her nan

THERE COULD ONLY BE ONE TULISA BECAUSE...
People love her glamorous style, her straight-talking and the way she plays mother hen to the boys

TULISA LOVES TO ...
Sing, act and go shopping with friends

MOST LIKELY TO SAY...
"I ain't feeling that!"

DID YOU KNOW?
Tulisa once confessed to getting a kick out of fishing with her dad. She has even dragged Dappy along, too!

STYLE FILE TULISA

When it comes to looking her best, Tulisa always dresses to impress! The boys in the band might grumble that she spends hours getting ready, but when the star does finally make an entrance, everybody stands back to enjoy the view. As far as Tulisa is concerned, style is all about feeling confident and making the very best of yourself.

When it's time to go out clubbing or perform, the star loves to go girlie. Her favourite colour is pink, working the shade in cute mini skirts, fitted corsets and bandeau dresses. Despite her fame, the clothes don't have to be designer – when Tulisa hits the mall, she refuses to pay more than around £50 for an item. As far as she's concerned, anyone can look classy without spending a fortune.

Tulisa believes in total grooming – from the top of her coiffured locks down to her perfectly manicured toes. Now that she's an *X Factor* judge, every appearance has to be a fashion statement! But despite the glamorous photos you might have seen in glossy magazines, Tulisa doesn't dress up to the nines every day. In real life she chills out in trainers and tracksuits, just like any other girl of her age.

"For me, I'm either slobbing about or going out, so I have two extremes. On a lazy day I normally wear leggings, Ugg boots and long T-shirts. Maybe a thick hoody if it's cold."

GET THE LOOK

- Break the rules by teaming girlie frills and killer heels.

- Cinch in waists with statement belts.

- Use styling tongs to ring the changes with your hair.

- Go *X Factor* in playsuits, asymmetric tops and mesh sandals.

GETTING TO KNOW...
FAZER

FULL NAME
Richard Rawson

NICKNAMES
Fazer

DATE OF BIRTH
5th February 1987

PLACE OF BIRTH
Camden Town, London

EYE COLOUR
Brown

FAVE FOOD
Anything West Indian

THERE COULD ONLY BE ONE FAZER BECAUSE...
No one works the sunglasses look better or can match his easy laid-back charm – and his famous eye for the ladies!.

DAPPY LOVES TO...
Rap, produce music, play football

MOST LIKELY TO SAY...
"Four hundred per cent!"

DID YOU KNOW?
Fazer loves connecting with his fans. He still runs his MySpace, Bebo, Facebook and Twitter pages from home!

STYLE FILE FAZER

Fazer's style is the essence of relaxed, urban cool – Adidas trainers, layered chains and retro polo shirts. Right from the early days, the star's approach to fashion has been to keep things low key and laid back. During interviews Fazer often pulls his cap down over his face, happy to let his bandmates soak up the spotlight. And whilst Dappy loves hats, Fazer has his own calling card – his distinctive dark glasses.

Whatever he wears, Fazer wears it well, dressing to suit his chilled-out personality. When he goes on stage, the rapper and DJ usually opts for black, stepping out in high-necked jackets, hooded tops and baggy jeans. It's all about 'no-effort' effort – Fazer looks good without even trying.

It seems however, that Fazer's style might be all set to change. When he's not working on N-Dubz tunes, he's busy recording material for his first solo album. Laying down his own tracks has given the star a whole new perspective on fashion!

"I go into the studio now in a three-piece suit with a bow tie as it makes me feel special. It's a frame-of-mind thing. If I feel like a million pounds that's what I'm going to execute."

Fazer understands that fashion choices can shape your look, image and even your attitude. Whether he selects a sharp suit or streetwear, the star can be guaranteed to work his style to the max!

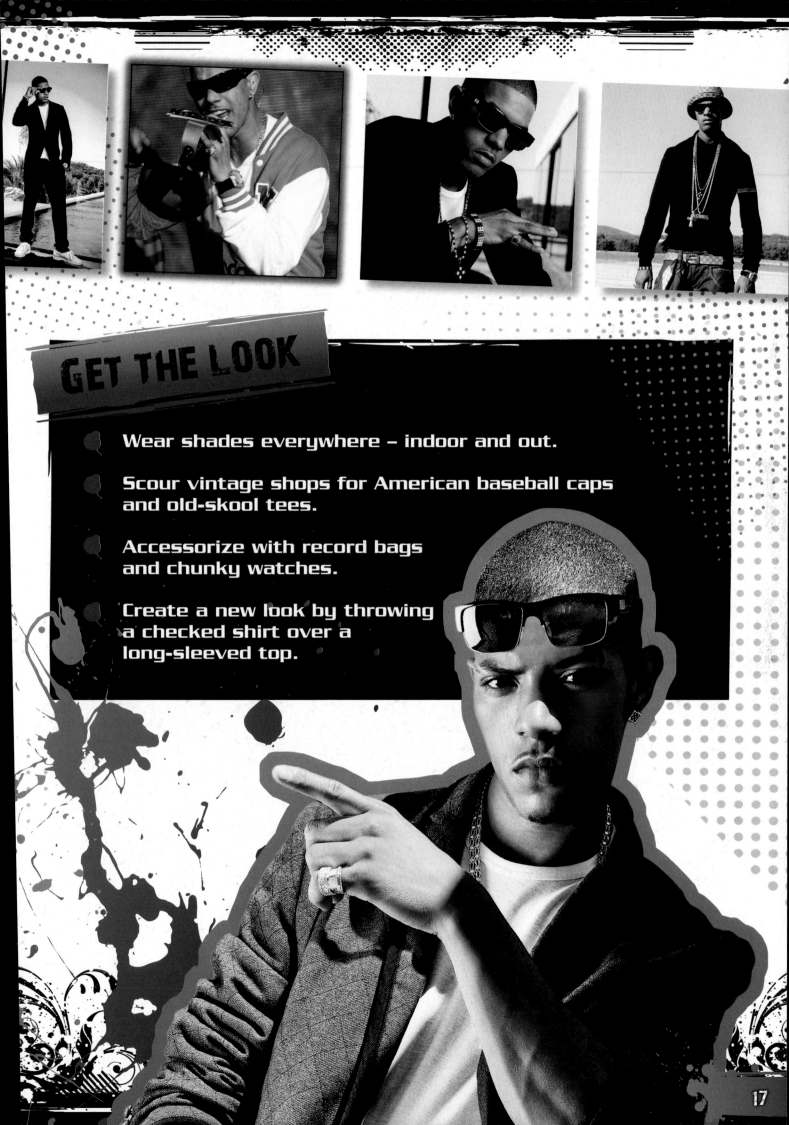

GET THE LOOK

- Wear shades everywhere – indoor and out.

- Scour vintage shops for American baseball caps and old-skool tees.

- Accessorize with record bags and chunky watches.

- Create a new look by throwing a checked shirt over a long-sleeved top.

SAY IT LIKE IT IS !

Neither Dappy, Fazer nor Tulisa is slow in giving an opinion! How well have you been listening? Read through these band quotes, then decide who said what.

WARNING

Read each conversation starter carefully – there are a few red herrings!

1 "We're not narrow-minded you get me, we can make big tunes, and we can make massive hooks, big concepts. That's why we've got Gary Barlow in. It ain't Take That, it's Take Braaaap."

Fazer ◯ Dappy ◯ Tulisa ◯ Not Dubz ◯

2 "The songs are like our children and we're very protective over them."

Fazer ◯ Dappy ◯ Tulisa ◯ Not Dubz ◯

3 "I'm more the one that sits there with my iPod on the rest of the time when I'm not on stage."

Fazer ◯ Dappy ◯ Tulisa ◯ Not Dubz ◯

4 "We want 50 Cent, Lil Wayne, Black Eyed Peas to say, 'Man, N-Dubz, they're the dogs!'"

Fazer ◯ Dappy ◯

Tulisa ◯ Not Dubz ◯

5 "I'm big into fishing, Dizzee Rascal got me in to it."

Fazer ◯ Dappy ◯

Tulisa ◯ Not Dubz ◯

6 "There's a big market out there for urban music and it still hasn't been opened one hundred per cent, and that's what we're trying to do."

Fazer ◯ Dappy ◯ Tulisa ◯ Not Dubz ◯

7 "Ten years of arguing is enough. We've stopped. It's been a month now."

Fazer ◯ Dappy ◯ Tulisa ◯ Not Dubz ◯

8 "I've had the whole of Fulham Youth Club outside my house for a week."

Fazer ◯ Dappy ◯ Tulisa ◯ Not Dubz ◯

9 "The more money you make, the less you have to pay for things."

Fazer ⬤ Dappy ⬤ Tulisa ⬤ Not Dubz ⬤

10 "Am I rich? I think I am! A little bit. Money makes it easier and there's no point saying it doesn't."

Fazer ⬤ Dappy ⬤ Tulisa ⬤ Not Dubz ⬤

11 "I used to say 'Niiiii' at least fifty times a day. I'm trying to cut back on that, no more than twenty a day now. It's under control!"

Fazer ⬤ Dappy ⬤ Tulisa ⬤ Not Dubz ⬤

12 "You've got to be polite, in't you? You've got to have manners."

Fazer ⬤ Dappy ⬤ Tulisa ⬤ Not Dubz ⬤

13 "Other people around the world, if we say, 'Get dahn!', well, they're going to say, 'What's he talking about?'"

Fazer ⬤ Dappy ⬤ Tulisa ⬤ Not Dubz ⬤

14 "Our fans are varied and that's a brilliant thing. I love that we appeal to all ages. We've got five-year-old fans that listen to our songs and then grandparents too!"

Fazer ⬤ Dappy ⬤ Tulisa ⬤ Not Dubz ⬤

15 "You know it's a game. You have to play it. There's always stories that are exaggerated, but you have to roll with it and laugh. It's entertainment."

Fazer ⬤ Dappy ⬤ Tulisa ⬤ Not Dubz ⬤

Are you an N-Dubz expert? Turn to page 92 and check your answers.

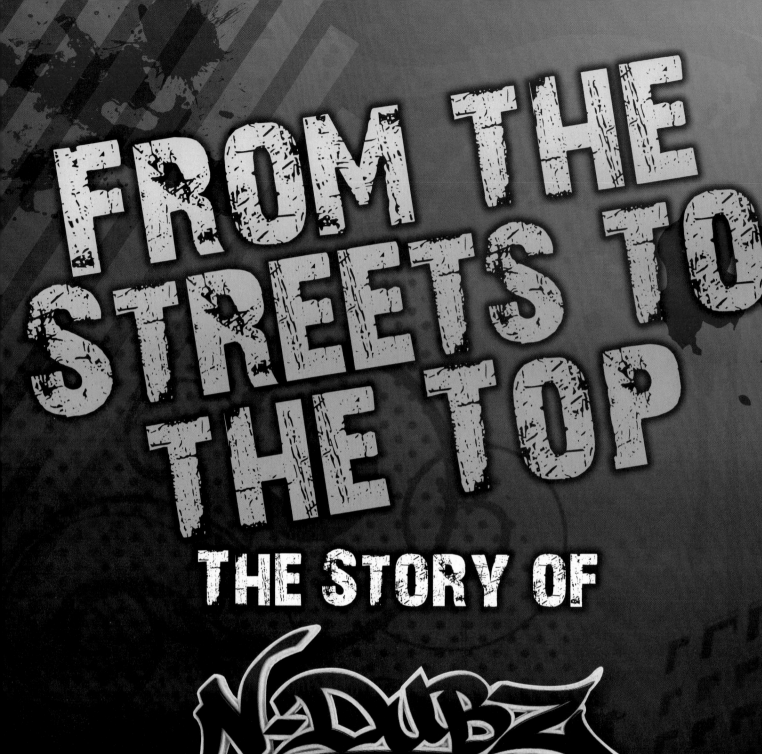

FROM THE STREETS TO THE TOP

THE STORY OF

N-DUBZ

PART 1

"I saw one, a fan, with a tattoo," Dappy explains, "...of my face! My face! On someone's arm. It's absolutely great!"

Quick question: How do three friends from London go from being regular inner city teenagers to one of the biggest bands in Europe, with images of their faces tattooed on their fan's bodies? And how can they achieve their dreams, but do it all on their own terms?

Answer: They become N-Dubz!

The band's incredible rise to the top began in 1987, in north London, Camden Town. On the 5th February, Richard Rawson was born to a Jamaican mother and English father. Soon after, on 11th June, musician Byron Contostavlos and partner Zoi Agorou welcomed their son Costas Dinos to the world. A little over a year later Byron was celebrating again, this time the arrival of his niece, Tula Contostavlos.

So far, so normal...

Growing up in Camden Town, the group lived a normal but tough life during their early years. Dappy, then known by a different nickname, Dino, attended Richard Cobden Primary School with his older brother, Spiros. Meanwhile, Fazer, or Richard as he was then, spent his early years living with his parents in a council flat on a rundown estate.

But it was Tulisa who had perhaps the hardest start in life. Her mother Anne was diagnosed with an illness that made her suffer from severe mood swings. She would go from being happy to depressed very quickly and without warning. Her condition was so serious she needed constant care.

> **"The doctors didn't seem to be able to stabilise my mum's moods. Music and my dream of becoming a success was all that kept me going through those very dark times. "**
>
> **Tulisa**

Tulisa lived with both her parents on the outskirts of Camden until they separated. When her dad moved out, she was forced to become her mum's full-time carer, responsible for looking after her all of the time. Tulisa was only nine years old.

While Tulisa's home life had forced her to learn to grow
up fast, her cousin Dappy was dealing with his own set o
problems. After attending the Richard Cobden Primary Sch
he moved up to an all-boys secondary school in nearby
Islington. He wasn't there for long.

After just a year, Dappy was expelled for truancy and wa
forced to join another new school, this time Camden's B:
Douglass School. Despite being given the chance of a fr
start, his behaviour went from bad to worse.

> **" I can't remember school too well; I wasn't there of**
>
> **Dappy**

Moving schools was a tough experience for Dappy. Being
kid he was a target for bullies and troublemakers, and
admitted he got into fights "...almost every day. It al
started with someone making fun of me or something stu

But, while Dappy's time inside the school gates wasn't
outside he'd already met the person destined to be his

Looking for an interest outside of their council estate, Richard Rawson's parents enrolled him in a local karate club when he was nine years old. As luck would have it, young Costas Dinos Contostavlos' parents had had the very same idea.

After meeting and realising that they were into the same stuff, the pair quickly became best mates. Fazer and Dappy shared karate moves, friends and the streets — but it was their passion for music that created a bond for life!

For Fazer and Dappy, music represented more than just a means of expressing themselves; it offered them a way out. Music gave them a chance to get away from their tough lives on the streets, and the opportunity to stay out of trouble.

> **" Me and Dappy were on the wrong path. Music is the saviour for us. "**
>
> **Fazer**

The pair quickly began writing rhymes and swapping song ideas. Even at this age, they knew that their connection was producing something special.

But, while they were delighted with the songs and the sound they were creating together, they also knew something was missing. Something, or someone...

24

Dappy's musical talent can be credited to the influence of his dad, Byron, who'd once been a member of the successful 70s' band Mungo Jerry. But it wasn't just Dappy — Tulisa had a musical background, too. While her dad Steve also played with Mungo Jerry, Tulisa's mum Anne and grandad were both musician

> ❝ My grandad was in a band. He always sang 'Molly Malone' to me. That's where I get my music from. ❞
> Tulisa

Fazer and Dappy were thirteen when they worked out what their songs and sound were lacking — balance. They knew that to get their music to as many people as possible, their tunes needed big hooks and an even bigger voice to sing them.

Luckily, they didn't have to look far. Tulisa had by now started attending the same school, Haverstock in Chalk Farm. The boys had heard Dappy's little cuz sing at family get-togethers. It didn't take long for them to decide that she had the voice they were looking for.

The band was born! But before they could begin their plans for world domination, they needed a name...

Dappy, Fazer and Tulisa weren't N-Dubz just yet. At just thirteen years old, the trio became the Likkle Rinsers Crew and set about taking over the charts! The band began performing around their local area.

While the threesome were busy turning their friends into fans and making a name for themselves, they also caught the imagination of someone who was to become the crew's inspiration and mentor — Byron Contostavlos.

"All that dedication and discipline was Uncle B. All of it."
Dappy

Of course, Byron was Dappy's dad, but he had also been a successful musician in his own right. He understood how bands break into the big-time. Byron, who the band called Uncle B, knew that talent could only take people so far.

To succeed the trio was going to need some luck, but more importantly, they had to be prepared to work for fame. To really make it, Uncle B said that Dappy, Fazer and Tulisa would have to work harder and longer than everyone else put together...

With Uncle B as their manager and mentor, the Likkle Rins[...]
Crew began hitting their local scene. They played anywher[...]
that would have them. They appeared in school halls and [...]
centres, at youth clubs and local talent competitions, a[...]
as throwing down impromptu freestyles and staging rap ba[...]
in the school playground.

While their music career was starting to take shape, thi[...]
at school and home weren't so good. With all their focus [...]
making it as a band, Dappy and Fazer often landed themse[...]
in trouble. They played truant from school and stayed o[...]
till late at night.

> **"Sometimes there were nights where my mum woul[...]
> be crying and begging me not to go out – but I ignor[...]
> her. I wanted to be able to get my own money and
> pay for my own things. I didn't really see that I wa[...]
> making her into an emotional wreck."**
>
> **Dappy**

Eventually, of course, things came to a head. Dappy le[...]
full-time education when he was fifteen years old, befo[...]
his exams. This was a decision he regretted, but he c[...]
it later when he returned to college to finish his GCS[...]

Just as the band were starting to see the pay-off from all their hard work, Dappy and Fazer's trouble-making spiralled out of control. Tulisa was spending more time away from the band caring for her mum, leaving the boys free to make a name for themselves in all the wrong ways.

> **"We were naughty! Me and Fazer, we used to go out on the streets and cause madness."**
> Dappy

> **"Me and Dappy were on the wrong path."**
> Fazer

Not for the first time, Dappy's dad, Uncle B, came to the rescue. He explained to the pair that they could have everything they wanted. They could have success, fans, fame and respect. But to get it there could be no cut-corners and no mistakes. They needed to focus their energy in the right way and stay on the straight and narrow. The band could fulfill their dream, but they couldn't afford to mess up!

So the question for Dappy and Fazer became simple. How much did they want it?

Turn to page 36 to find out how the Likkl

Fazer and Dappy decided to get focused. With the band turning in some great live performances, it was time to start making recordings. Any money they earned from their early gigs was put back into the cost of laying down demos.

As well as managing the band, Uncle B also worked in a local barbers. He used any extra money that he made to buy equipment so the Likkle Rinsers Crew could set up a home studio. He encouraged Dappy, Fazer and Tulisa to experiment with their sound. Soon they were learning the skills they needed to produce professional music.

> " He put every last penny into rehearsals and studio. If it wasn't for him we'd be dead or in jail – we owe it all to B. "
> **Dappy**

Their fans couldn't get enough of each new track. Tunes like 'Bad Man Riddim' and 'Life Is Getting Sicker By The Day' were now not just a hit during gigs, they were also winning over new fans on local radio stations!

People were starting to notice the Likkle Rinsers Crew. After years of developing their skills, stardom finally seemed within their grasp. But there were to be a few more twists and turns ahead for Dappy, Fazer and Tulisa...

Rinsers Crew transformed into N-Dubz!

IT'S A WHOLE NEW SLANGUAGE!

Banging albums like 'Against All Odds' are packed with a string of words and phrases that you won't hear anywhere else. Over the years, N-Dubz have developed a street slang that is totally unique to them! Each phrase is cool, fizzing in attitude and totally authentic.

What would you say to the band if you bumped into them on the street? Study this official dictionary, learn the catchphrases and – *boom!* – you'll be talking N-Dubz in no time...

"NaNaNiiiii"
Official N-Dubz trademark

"Minkie"
Cute

"N-Dublet"
N-Dubz fan

"Are u suuuuuuuick"
That's amazing

"DAP's"
Short version of Dappy

"Ha Ha"
Official N-Dubz trademark

"Peng"
fit, good-looking

"Weeeeeeeeeeeeeee!"
The chuffed cry you make when you've shown someone up

"Maddas 4 rallies"
That's totally mad

"Zoop Zoop"
An expression of excitement

"Duku Yourself"
Big up yourself

"Seari 4 realli"
Are you serious?

"Say something"
End of conversation

"Bang bang shoes"
Nice shoes

"Pickney"
Little kid

"D-A-P's to the Y"
Dappy

"NaNa"
Hi and/or goodbye

"F A take it easy"
Fazer

"TT"
Tulisa

"Shabarky"
Somebody's eyeing you up

"Pinky"
A £50 note

DISCOGRAPHY

In five short years, N-Dubz have released an impressive list of records. In addition to three platinum albums, the Camden Town kids have kept the singles coming thick and fast – each one offering a fresh take on the essential N-Dubz sound. In the future America beckons, and so there are sure to be even more banging tunes to get the fans up on their feet!

THE ALBUMS

2008 Uncle B

2009 Against All Odds

2010 Love. Live. Life

THE SINGLES

2006
- You Better Not Waste My Time
- I Swear

2007
- Feva Las Vegas

2008
- Ouch
- Papa Can You Hear Me?

2009
- Strong Again
- Wouldn't You
- I Need You
- Playing With Fire (feat. Mr Hudson)

- Number 1 (Tinchy Stryder feat. N-Dubz)
- I Got Soul (as Young Soul Rebels for War Child)
- Lose My Life (Chipmunk feat. N-Dubz)

2010
- Say It's Over
- We Dance On (feat. Bodyrox)
- Best Behaviour
- Girls

2011
- Morning Star
- So Alive (Skepta vs. N-Dubz)
- Stuttering (Loick Essien feat. N-Dubz)

VIDEOS IN THE MIX

Their schedules are beyond hectic, but N-Dubz have still found the time to appear in a staggering 27 music videos! This page features six of the best. Read the vision behind each release, get a feel for the vibe and then draw a line to match it to the track it was made for.

1 The band deliver a tune from the heart. Dappy, Tulisa and Fazer float in front of a gently rolling sunset, while people look on holding candles.

A I Swear

2 A helicopter lands with Dappy inside, Fazer appears on a superbike and Tulisa steps out of a fast car. As the track unfolds, the trio are shown in a club – each one proving unlucky in love.

B Papa Can You Hear Me?

3 The band team up with a very special guest for a night shoot on location in London town. A suspicious Tulisa is also shown checking her boyfriend's texts while he sleeps in bed beside her, leading the song to a heart-rending hook.

C Best Behaviour

4 Dappy confronts a dude that has been playing away with his girlfriend in a tune loaded with blame and denial. The video includes a gritty confrontation underneath a canal bridge.

D I Need You

5 A cool cast of kids present how Dappy, Tulisa and Fazer might have looked when they were young. The awesome dance-off sequence is intercut with clips from the movie *StreetDance*.

E Playing With Fire

6 The band's private jet brings the N-Dubz back from tour. Each of the crew drops their personalised Louis Vuitton luggage outside their door. Yet despite the super-luxe setting, Dappy, Fazer and Tulisa's performance is full of regret.

F We Dance On

FROM THE STREETS TO THE TOP
THE STORY OF

PART 2

Thanks to their explosive live shows and a growing reputation for producing great tracks in the studio, things were going well for Fazer, Dappy and Tulisa. Music industry big-wigs were starting to take notice of what was happening in Camden! But despite their success, the Likkle Rinsers Crew's days were numbered.

Fazer, Dappy and Tulisa weren't kids any more. They were growing up, and it was time to change their name to something that suited them better. To reflect the pride they felt in the area they came from, the crew started calling themselves NW1, Camden Town's postcode. It wasn't long before this was shortened to N-Dubz.

> " We are far from an overnight success. There was no X-Factor-style standing in a queue to become famous for us. "
>
> **Dappy**

With a new name and a loyal and eager fan base, the record companies couldn't ignore the band any longer! The N-Dubz quickly signed their first record deal. Work started on Dappy, Fazer and Tulisa's debut album.

Just as the band's dreams were coming true, tragedy struck. On 12th April 2007 Byron Contostavlos, N-Dubz's manager, mentor and inspiration died suddenly at home of a heart attack. The band were devastated, but threw themselves into their work.

Taking heed of all the lessons Uncle B had taught them about hard work and focus, N-Dubz kept rolling. The following evening, the band performed for 2,000 fans in London. Work continued on their first album and the threesome used the loss of Uncle B to write one of their first breakthrough hits, 'Papa Can You hear Me?'

" It was the lowest point in our lives, we had no money, no manager, no driver, no accountant, but most of all, I had no father – B was everything to me and it hurts so much to think that he never got to see what we have achieved now, but I know he's looking down on us and he'd be really proud. "
Dappy

Before his tragic death, Byron had told the band that their first album should be called 'Against All Odds', to mark the crew's unlikely rise to fame. Now the band had a different idea.

On the 17th November 2008 N-Dubz released their debut album. It was simply called 'Uncle B'.

By now there was no stopping N-Dubz. Their music was flying off the shelves! The industry was taking note, too. In 2007, the guys won the Best Newcomer award at the MOBOs. They were nominated in two categories at the 2008 Urban Music Awards. A year later, they won two more MOBOs, for Best UK Act and the prestigious Best Album award. The arrival of 2010 brought them another MOBO, this time for Best Song, and a Brit Award nomination.

> " Whatever achievements we get, we just keep on going. Getting the two best awards at the MOBOs was awesome, but there's no stopping there. We want a Brit now. "
>
> **Dappy**

After years of trying, the band had finally made it. N-Dubz was here to stay!

The band had successfully won over the music industry.
People were queuing up to work with the band and N-Dubz
were only too happy to oblige!

Seizing the opportunity to expand their sound and learn
from other successful artists, the band's studio had an
open-door policy. As the big name acts came in, the hits
came rolling out.

> **" I thank God that we are doing this. Who would of
> thought we would be selling out venues, collaborating
> with amazing artists and selling over 400,000 albums?
> We are so grateful. "**
>
> **Fazer**

Big names like Mr Hudson, Tinchy Stryder, Gary Barlow and
Chipmunk have all shared studio space with Dappy, Tulisa and
Fazer. And, with artists like Kylie Minogue and Katy Perry
rumoured to be keen to collaborate with them, the future
looked even brighter!

Now they'd become an established recording act with a ton of cool tracks to perform, the band hit the road. This time the venues were a little bigger than the school halls and local London spots that they'd played all those years ago!

N-Dubz headed out around Europe with an explosive live show. Dappy, Fazer and Tulisa were playing arenas now and, despite the huge crowds, they still managed to find a way to connect with each and every fan in the place.

> **" Some fans ask whether they can touch me and it's like I have an electric current going through my body because when I touch them they start going crazy and screaming."**
>
> **Fazer**

After years of knock-backs, broken promises and false starts, N-Dubz had made it. Their music was at the top of the charts, their tours sold out, they were regularly collaborating with respected artists and were gathering an impressive collection of awards. Dappy, Fazer and Tulisa were sitting at the top, but guess who couldn't sit still?

Not for the first time in their career, N-Dubz took a risk. On the 21st June 2010 the band let the world take a look behind the scenes of their lives in their reality show *Being... N-Dubz*. In an industry where images are carefully managed and looking your best in public at all times is a job requirement, letting cameras film their every move could have been seen as a dangerous decision.

But for Dappy, Fazer and Tulisa, appearing on the show was simply an extension of what they were already doing. Uncle B had always taught them the value of being true to themselves and only writing and singing about what they know. The crew's music had always acknowledged their bad points as well as their good ones — they took pride in keeping things real.

Being... N-Dubz showed the band, warts and all. Fans got to see everything, including the fiery relationship between Tulisa and Dappy. The cousins regularly argued in the way only family can!

> ❝ We've made a pact. Ten years of arguing is enough. We've stopped. I did a Dappy tattoo, as a pact of goodwill. ❞
>
> Tulisa

Funny, interesting and, above all, real, the show was an instant success. *Being... N-Dubz* was quickly signed up for a second series.

With N-Dubz, fans have learnt to expect the unexpected. When Simon Cowell, Cheryl Cole and Dannii Minogue announced that they were leaving *The X Factor* judging panel in 2011, the show's producers knew they needed big names with great experience to take their place.

Take That main man Gary Barlow was drafted in, along with former Destiny's Child star Kelly Rowland and returning judge Louis Walsh. The producers needed one more judge to complete the line-up. They wanted someone fresh who had made it in the music industry — someone who could use their experience to spot the same talent and drive in others. They found exactly who they were looking for in Tulisa.

> ❝ **I'm really nervous. I feel pressure, but I don't feel like I'm stepping into anyone's shoes because I could never be Cheryl or Dannii.** ❞
> **Tulisa**

Tulisa was an instant success with auditionees, crowds and judges alike. Louis Walsh was quick to praise her. "Tulisa has fitted in to the panel so well," he told a newspaper. "There is a great dynamic now. She has that girl-next-door appeal that Cheryl had and I'd say she's even better!"

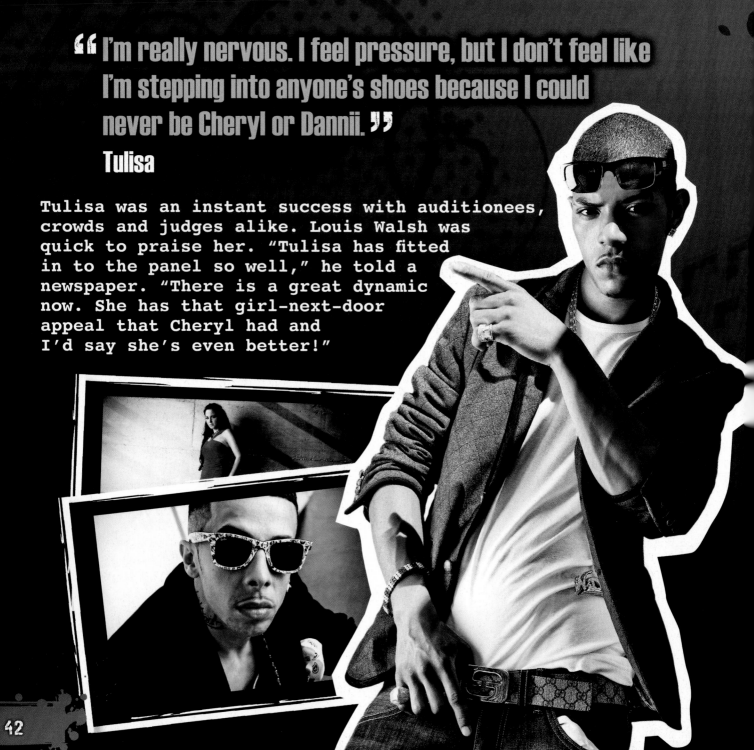

RHYME TIME

Since bursting on to the scene, N-Dubz have become famous for the stories they tell and pictures they paint with their lyrics. It really is all about the music! Now the time has come to test your N-Dublet credentials. Read the rhymes then write the correct song title underneath.

1. "Yesterday morning, coming home at 5.34, the final show was cancelled. I'm back early from tour."

Song? ....

2. "See me I made a change, I didn't expect no fame, we came from practically nuttin' to thousands screaming our name."

Song? ....

3. "I ain't gonna lie, Mama tried the best to bring me up right, guess it never worked, she cries. I was always involved in crime, from the age of nine."

Song? ....

4. "If you've got your own whip and you're earning paper, then you have the right to be a heartbreaker."

Song? ....

5. "Cos I'm such good liar, just admit it, I never did it, yes you did it, no I didn't, ayy."

Song? ....

6. "When the revolution comes, I'm going dressed up as a soldier, put my arm and run and I won't sleep until it's over, let me show ya."

Song? ....

7. "Ohhhh, you can be my biggest fan, never let me go, I'm gonna go harder then I ever did before."

Song? ....

8. "See I need some kind of man that, that can understand that the female boss is who I have to be."

Song? ....

9. "What would I do without you? What would you do without me? Don't need to tell you baby coz it's plain for us to see."

Song? ....

10. "There ain't a way in the world it's how I thought this would end up. If it wasn't for you B, there wouldn't be N-Dubz."

Song? ....

Lost for words? The ten song titles are jumbled up in this word box. Match the right one to the right tune and you're on course for full marks!

NA NA   LOVE FOR MY SLUM

NO ONE KNOWS

PLAYING WITH FIRE

BEST BEHAVIOUR

I SWEAR

PAPA CAN YOU HEAR ME?

STRONG AGAIN   GIRLS   SCREAM MY NAME

NW1 WORDSERCH

Dappy, Fazer and Tulisa are so proud of being residents of Camden Town, they even named their crew after its London postcode! NW1 is an area teeming with famous landmarks, amazing markets and brilliant music venues.

Ten cool Camden locations have been hidden in this wordsearch grid. Can you track them all down? Don't blink – the words could be running in any direction, even back to front!

```
D H K K I L O S F X T M
J D R E W O T T B B E O
R E G R N T S P A R K O
O T G P W C V A H K R R
U O V M M E J N E P A L
N A Z E M I Z W C D S M L
D D M N K S L R J M N A
H S I N O P A A A X E B
O E T X K D S R X V D C
U G Y L O W N E D F M I
S J F V J Q D O O T A R
E A E R A K C O L T C T
Q P X V M B V G S D G C
D U B L I N C A S T L E
L G H A B R C A E I P L
U E P X Z S Q L B M M E
```

**CAMDEN MARKET ELECTRIC BALLROOM REGENTS PARK
KOKO BT TOWER DUBLIN CASTLE LOCK AREA
LONDON ZOO ROUNDHOUSE ST PANCRAS**

PAPPED!

The press are always tailing N-Dubz, hoping to get a good picture! Take a close look at this shot of the band posing in an exotic new location. The photo below it was never used – study it carefully and then circle six reasons why not.

HIGHS AND LOWS

Being part of N-Dubz is like riding a rollercoaster – over the years Dappy, Fazer and Tulisa have experienced both champagne-popping triumphs and heart-wrenching lows. Thanks to their positive attitude, the band have proved they can benefit just as much from the good times as they can from the bad...

Beating the odds

Despite their tough beginnings, the band have won over the music industry and transformed themselves into a household name. N-Dubz never take no for an answer and though all three members of the band have faced obstacles, they've showed that with determination and hard work you can achieve your dreams!

Uncle B

Just as the band were hitting the big time, their manager, mentor and Dappy's father, Uncle B, tragically died. Although they were all devastated, the crew showed they could turn even the worst negative into a positive by using Uncle B's memory as the inspiration for their career.

An award-winning band

After winning over record company bosses and a legion of fans, the band started receiving praise and awards from their peers. To date they have been nominated for several Brit and Urban Music awards and won a Silver Clef award plus an incredible four MOBOs!

Controversy

Nobody, not even N-Dubz, is perfect! It hasn't all been plain-sailing for the band since they made it famous. Dappy, Fazer and Tulisa have found their name in the papers for the wrong reasons on several occasions. However, keeping true to their positive image, each time the band have slipped up they have always been quick to admit to their errors, advising fans not to make the same mistakes that they have.

Number 1

A chart-topping record would have seemed a long way away for Dappy, Fazer and Tulisa when they put the band together in 2000. But they achieved the incredible feat when they teamed up with Tinchy Stryder on the track 'Number 1'. Not bad going for three kids from Camden!

Being N-Dubz

Having your own reality TV show would be a high point in anyone's career. But rather than celebrating, N-Dubz view their success in the show based on what they have been able to learn from it. The band got a chance to take a step back and see their usual bickering and arguing from an outside point of view. Dappy and Tulisa promised to work hard to improve their relationship after seeing the show. Now the band are stronger than ever.

Solo success

Being in the band has also brought Dappy, Tulisa and Fazer individual rewards. While N-Dubz takes a well-deserved break, each member is now busy with their own projects. Forget taking a holiday, the guys are still bringing the famous N-Dubz work ethic to their new endeavours! Dappy is embarking on a solo career and releasing his own music. Fazer has moved behind the scenes to produce music for other artists – there are even whispers that one could be US pop sensation Katy Perry. Tulisa, meanwhile, has been confirmed as one of the four judges on the new series of *The X Factor*.

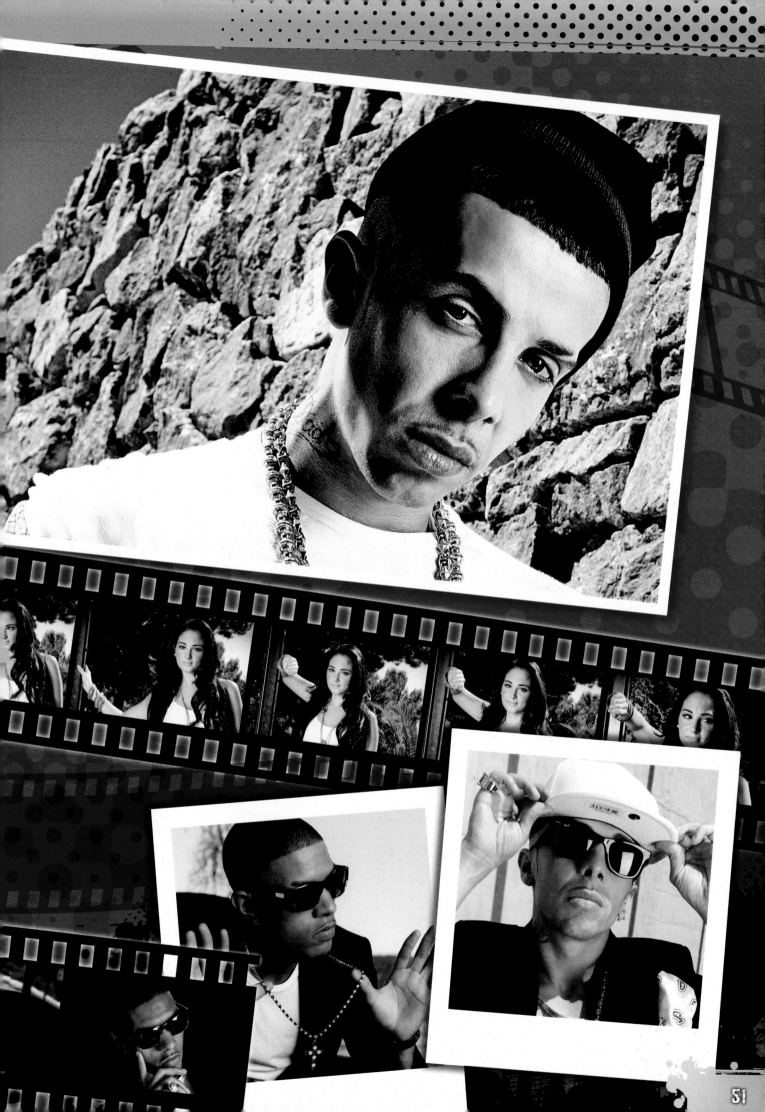

READ ALL ABOUT IT

Appearing in the papers comes with the territory when you're in a band as successful as N-Dubz. Hardly a day goes by without one of the band having a story written about them in the tabloids. Are you up to date with the latest N-Dubz media hype? Scan the headlines below, then decide if you think they're real or fake.

FAZER FURIOUS WITH DAPPY'S DEMANDS

Real as it gets ○
Faked for fun ○

TULISA'S A HIT IN SUMMER BLOOM!

Real as it gets ○   Faked for fun ○

N-DUBZ BLAST CHEATING ARTISTS

Real as it gets ○   Faked for fun ○

IT'S END-DUBZ!

Real as it gets ○   Faked for fun ○

CONTESTANT TELLS TULISA: 'DUBZ BE GOOD TO ME'

Real as it gets ○
Faked for fun ○

PRINCE CHARLES APPROVES OF N-DUBZ TRIO

Real as it gets ○
Faked for fun ○

TULISA TOLD OFF FOR PARTYING

7

Real as it gets ○
Faked for fun ○

FAZER FIRED UP FOR KYLIE COLLABORATION

8

Real as it gets ○   Faked for fun ○

TULISA 'SO EXCITED' TO LAND REBECCA BLACK DUET

9

Real as it gets ○
Faked for fun ○

DERMOT O'LEARY RESCUES TULISA FROM 'CHAVS' WHO MOB HER

10

Real as it gets ○
Faked for fun ○

N-DUBZ DAPPY JOINS THE SATURDAYS

11

Real as it gets ○
Faked for fun ○

DAPPY WOULD 'LOVE TO WORK WITH PHIL COLLINS'

12

Real as it gets ○   Faked for fun ○

FAZER PENS FOR KATY PERRY

Real as it gets ○   Faked for fun ○

13

BIG UP TO N-DUBZ!

As soon as they hit the music scene, N-Dubz started picking up industry awards. The group have now been presented with an impressive stash of statue always taking the opportunity to thank the fans for their support along the way.

2007

MOBO Awards
Best Newcomer – Winner

The MOBOs were the first awards show in Europe to celebrate and champion urban music.

2008

Urban Music Awards
Best Group – Nominated

Best Music Video
'Ouch' – Nominated

The Urban Music Awards is the premiere R&B, hip-hop, soul and dance music awards ceremony in the world.

2009

O2 Silver Clef Awards
The Digital Award – Winner

MOBO Awards
Best UK Act – Winner

Best Album
'Uncle B' – Winner

The O2 Silver Clef Awards are held every year to celebrate the very best in the industry and raise money to transform people's lives through music.

2010

BRIT Awards
British Single
'Number 1' – Nominated

The BRIT Awards is the UK's most prestigious music ceremony, attended by the cream of Britain's talent.

MOBO Awards
Best Song
'Playing With Fire' – Winner

STYLE IT OUT !

Getting ready for an award ceremony is a major deal, even for the N-Dubz boys! Dappy, Tulisa and Fazer pick out hot new looks to make them stand out from the A-list crowd.

Imagine that N-Dubz have been invited to a brand new music show. What should they wear? Grab a pen or pencil, then cast yourself as the crew's official stylist. Use these pages to draw the band members in the outfits that will make them look a million Duku dollars.

Don't forget to accessorize with snappy hats, bang bang shoes and bling!

DAPPY

TULISA

FAZER

MAKE YOUR MARK

Wanna be in a top band like N-Dubz? With some talent and a lot of hard work maybe you can! Whether you want to be in an urban pop group, a vocal duo or even a rock band, follow this guide to get yourself started on the path to superstardom.

GETTING STARTED

The first thing you need to do is decide what sort of crew you want to be. Take a look at your music collection and think about the albums and sounds that really excite you. No matter how big your band becomes and how many fans you have, no one should be more passionate about your music than you are.

FIND YOUR BAND MATES

In many ways, bands are like recipes. Some things taste great because their ingredients all have similar flavours, whilst others work because the individual elements are so different (who'd have thought that chocolate and chilli could combine as such a taste sensation?). When putting your band together, it's important to experiment with lots of different people. Ask your mates and family, see if your music teacher can recommend anyone and talk to kids that go to the same clubs. Try all sorts of flavours out and you'll soon find a recipe that works for you.

SET YOUR SOUND

N-Dubz is all about working together to come up with something fresh and unique. Take the time to listen to each other's ideas, even if you don't agree with them. Play your music to lots of people who aren't in the band, then take on board their praise and criticisms. Music is always changing – there are no limits, so don't be afraid to change your mind. And don't worry if it feels tricky. Just like every outfit in the world, finding and refining your sound is a journey your band will always be on.

KEEP IT REAL

There's one trick that all the best artists know. Don't worry, it's no big secret – just be yourself. Whether it's Eminem talking about his family problems, Dappy rapping about life in Camden Town or even Lady Gaga expressing her love for out-there fashion, it works because it's authentic. People will connect with you and your music if they feel that you're telling them the truth.

CHOOSE A NAME

So you've got a band, you're working on your music and you believe in what you're doing. Now you need to decide what to call yourselves. This can be a tough job, but don't let it stress you out. No matter what you choose, people very quickly forget the name – instead they remember the performers. Read books and magazines, think of meaningful song lyrics or follow N-Dubz's lead and seek inspiration in your local area. Write all your ideas down then have a brainstorming session with your band mates. You'll have a cool new identity in no time!

PRACTICE MAKES PERFECT

No one gets good at something overnight, it takes unswerving dedication. One of the most important lessons you can learn from N-Dubz's story is how hard the band worked to get to where they are today. Rehearse at each other's houses, meet up and practice at school, freestyle in the shower, or even just run through the songs in your own mind. The trick is not to make it feel like a chore. If you're enjoying it, you'll soon notice the improvements.

GET OUT THERE

Your next step is to take your music to the people. It can be nerve-wracking showing off your songs, but it's something every band have to do. Make up demo tapes, check local youth clubs and music shops to see if there are any talent shows coming up or ask a parent to help you put on your own show. It'll be scary at first, but you'll love the adrenaline buzz that comes with performing live!

DON T GIVE UP

Making yourself a success is never easy and the music business is notorious for being one of the toughest industries out there. Ask any successful musician and they'll all confess to having had times when they've been rejected or passed over. Getting knocked back isn't the important thing, in fact it will make you a better artist. It's how you handle these bumps in the road that really matters.

BELIEVE IN YOURSELVES, WORK HARD AND YOU CAN DO IT!

ON THE ROAD

Whenever N-Dubz announce a new tour, it's always a sell-out! The band get a total kick from tearing up the stage, putting 400% into each and every show. Whenever the threesome confirm a new set of dates, they up the ante. Every show has to be bigger and better than the last!

Uncle B Tour

March – April 2009

These dates will always be special, because they were N-Dubz's first concerts as a signed band. Sixteen shows were originally booked, but five more had to be added because the fans wanted more! The guys were supported by Fe-Nix, Stevie Hoang and their pal Tinchy Stryder.

N-Dubz Christmas Party/ Clubland 3 Live

November – December 2009

N-Dubz kicked off their Christmas tour in Southend, performing most nights to packed concert halls up and down the UK. Halfway through the tour, the band took time out to semi-headline in the 'Clubland 3' event, sharing the stage with Cascada. Other acts included record labels mates Agnes, Frisco and Darren Styles.

Against All Odds Tour

March – September 2010

Despite appearing at over thirty venues, the band's third tour was another complete sell-out! N-Dubz got the crowds jumping with live renditions of tracks from their second album, plus a knockout cover of Script song 'The Man Who Can't Be Moved.'

Love. Live. Life. Tour

April – May 2011

Earlier this year, Dappy, Fazer and Tulisa treated the N-Dublets to their first ever arena tour. The N- Dubz tour bus visited fourteen cities including London, Dublin, Glasgow and Newcastle. The show was an amazing spectacle packed with pyrotechnics, tight dance sets and thumping hit songs.

The tour was originally planned to run through to the end of April, but due to unprecedented demand extra dates were added in Bristol, Leicester, Leeds, Liverpool and Oxford. N-Dubz rocked the houses, wowing crowds of 15,000 every night. Professor Green's support act added to the energy, as did a stomping encore featuring a mash-up of some of the band's most famous tunes. Suuuick!

Love. Live. Life
tour set list

Took It All The Away
Strong Again
Living for the Moment
Playing With Fire
I Swear
Girls
Toot It & Boot It
Acoustic covers: Meet Me Half Way (Black Eyed Peas)/Down (Jay Seans)
My Name is Tulisa
Love Sick
Scream My Name
Love. Live. Life
Morning Star
Say It's Over
Cold Shoulder
So Alive
Papa

Encore:

Medley of Defeat You, Love For My Slums, Better Not Waste My Time, Ouch, Sex, Number 1 (N-Dubz Remix) Best Behaviour

LIFE ON TOUR

"The travelling is amazing. You're on the tour bus having jokes, living from hotel to hotel and you never know what the next city is going to have for you."

Dappy

"Life on the road isn't always fun for me because I'm the only chick! We travel separately because we'd actually kill each other if we travelled together. Those two go on the tour bus and I follow in a car and stay in hotels."

Tulisa

"I don't really have a pre-show ritual to get myself hyped up. I've been doing it for so long that I'm just kind of ready. The only thing I do really is start jumping up and down on the spot to get my adrenaline going."

Fazer

"I know what I'm all about on stage and I'm like a switch. The minute I put my show clothes on and my Dappy hat, that's it. I'm the showman. I limber up, do my little stretches from karate and then bound on stage because I know what the fans want.'

Dappy

"The buzz on stage is amazing if I relax and allow myself to enjoy it. Sometimes I get too caught up in worrying about looking and sounding right. When I let loose, that's when I enjoy it most. It's one of the best feelings in the world."
Tulisa

"Seeing 10,000 people singing your vocal back to you without you even saying anything is the most overwhelming feeling that you could ever have."
Fazer

RIDER REQUEST LIST

When the band arrive at each new venue, they ask for a few things to be ready and waiting in their dressing rooms. Even though they're massive, N-Dubz aren't divas — their list is made up of practical stuff to help them get dressed, psyched and fed before the show. Check out this list of the crew's backstage riders.

Clean towels

Speakers to play some sounds

Full-length mirrors

A sofa for pre-show chillaxing

Capri Sun drinks

Twiglets and McCoys crisps for when the munchies come

Nando's chicken

EVERYBODY SAY NANANIIII!

What will the next N-Dubz tour be like? After the explosive success of Love. Live. Life, it's going to be pretty tough to beat! Could there be a string of US dates waiting around the corner, or maybe even a massive world tour?

Imagine how the dynamic trio might present their next live appearance. What would they call the tour and what would the vibe be? Who might be supporting? When you've taken a call on it, design a knock-out N-Dubz tour poster to pin up all over town.

READ AND RHYME

Dappy and Fazer are constantly bouncing off each other, spitting lyrics and trying out new ideas. When they were young the boys would battle for hours, then go home and write more lines to try out the next day. Now the pair rap about life on the street, family, love – anything that feels important to them and comes straight from the heart.

Now it's your chance to think up a new lyric to rap. Use this page to rough out ideas and play with rhymes. Don't worry if you're not good at English. Just use your imagination and give it a try. If you focus, you'll be surprised at what you can do.

DUKU YOURSELF

N-DUBZ DEETS

Since coming together as a band, Tulisa, Dappy and Fazer have toured the world, recorded a mass of great music and graced the charts many times. Now it's time to do the numbers! This fierce stats quiz has been devised to challenge the toughest N-Dubz fan. Find a pen, get focused and then see how high you can score.

1/ How many full-length albums have the band released?

2/ The band's first single was called 'You Better Not Waste My Time'. Was it a top 40, top 30 or top 20 hit?

3/ How many times have N-Dubz been the featured artist on another act's single release?

4/ Tulisa is one of the judges on this year's *The X Factor*. How many judges are on the panel?

5/ In which year were both Fazer and Dappy born?

6/ How many children does Dappy have?

7/ To date, how many music videos have N-Dubz made?

8/ N-Dubz are big on Twitter. Do they have over 50,000, 100,000 or 200,000 followers?

9/ When Fazer is confident that something is sure to happen, he quotes a percentage. Do you know what that percentage is?

10/ How many nationwide tours have N-Dubz been on?

11/ The band have won numerous awards. How many MOBO accolades have they picked up so far?

12/ How many times have the band appeared on Radio 1's Live Lounge?

13/ The albums Uncle B and Against All Odds were both certified as platinum in the UK. How many copies do you need to sell to be awarded this status?

14/ In 2010 the band starred in their own reality TV show, *Being… N-Dubz*. How many episodes were there in the series?

15/ To the nearest 100,000, how many times was the official video for N-Dubz' Cold Shoulder viewed in its first three months on YouTube?

CREW CROSSWORD

This wicked crossword is packed with N-Dubz facts. Grab a pen, study the clues, then fill in the blanks. Can you cruise through the whole puzzle? Only true N-Dublets will be able to ace the whole square!

ACROSS

1. Early N-Dubz tune dedicated to their home town.
2. Music genre that influences Dappy's rapping style.
3. Fazer's real name.
4. Dappy's beloved dad and Tulisa's uncle.
5. Remix of a track featuring Skepta as a guest artist.
6. Top US rapper and producer that has inspired Dappy, Tulisa and Fazer's sound.

DOWN

1. Classic N-Dubz track featuring Mr Hudson.
2. The first award that the band scooped at the MOBOs.
3. The Mediterranean country where Dappy and Tulisa's roots lie.
4. Band slang for a fifty pound note.
5. N-Dubz tune that scored over 4,000,000 hits on YouTube.
6. Channel 4 drama with all three band members playing different roles.

LIVING THE DREAM

STARZ ON SCREEN

N-Dubz are so much more than an urban pop group! As well as working on a whole range of joint and solo projects, the guys can boast an impressive CV of television credits. From reality TV to serious acting, viewers can't get enough of Tulisa, Fazer and Dappy!

BEING N_DUBZ

In 2010 Adidas Originals sponsored a fascinating fly-on-the-wall documentary about the band. Each of the N-Dubz stars wore headcams, so that viewers could see the world through their eyes – literally. From trips back to Dappy and Fazer's hood, to live gigs and celebrity football matches, fans got to see the band live and un-cut. Whilst series one tracked the crew in and around the UK music scene, the second series followed their bid to crack the tough American market.

DUBPLATE DRAMA

'Dubplate Drama' is a cutting edge youth drama – not least because the N-Dubz are in it! Fêted as the world's first interactive television show, the C4 programme has now run into three series. Tulisa joined the cast as Laurissa in series two, with cameo roles for Dappy and Fazer. She performed so well in the emotional scenes that her part was expanded, becoming arch-rival to Dionne and one of the show's main characters. Since the last episode aired, there is even talk about bringing out a Dubplate Drama movie.

THE X FACTOR

Since Cheryl Cole left the last season of 'The X Factor', there has just been one name on everybody's lips – Tulisa Contoslavlos! The star hit the headlines when she landed the plum role, pulling up a chair on the judge's platform next to Kelly Rowland, Louis Walsh and old pal Gary Barlow! Will Tulisa be a harsh or sweet-talking critic? Only time will tell...

SECRETS OF SUCCESS

What advice do N-Dubz have for rising stars on the urban scene? The crew talk about the principles that have got them where they are today.

Fazer on his musical roots...

"The drive still comes from remembering where we started... We don't take it for granted and we know we have to work every day to deserve it."

DAPPY ON AIMING HIGH...

"YOU'RE CAPABLE OF DOING ANYTHING IN LIFE WITH TWO HANDS AND A BRAIN."

Dappy on staying true...

"Be a good person, be confident within yourself. Make sure you like the music that you do so that when you put it out, people see that and will be drawn in."

Dappy on always striving...

"Me and Fazer's motto is 'You have to keep on working.' We always need to get another number one, another smash, another big show."

Fazer on sticking together...

"Dappy and Tulisa come first. They're like family to me. If those two don't approve of something I wanna do in our business, it won't get done. Simple. We're a tripod and if one leg falls, we all fall."

Tulisa on keeping it personal...

"On some tracks one of us will write more than the others. Fazer makes up all the beats and I would say that Dappy writes sixty to seventy per cent of the hooks, but we all write our own verses."

TULISA ON MAKING MUSIC FROM HEART...

"MOST OF OUR TRACKS ARE STORIES – WE'RE NOT HERE TO CHAT A LOT OF GIBBERISH. I PERSONALLY THINK IT'S MUCH BETTER TO HAVE SOMETHING THAT PEOPLE CAN IDENTIFY WITH..."

DOING IT WITH DUBZ

Music has always been about mixing things up for N-Dubz! The crew have made hits with a sparkling array of stars during their career, from class rapper Tinchy Stryder to writing legend Gary Barlow. Here's a few of the best...

Artist — Tinchy Stryder
Song — Number 1

Rapper Tinchy Stryder worked with the band on what would be their first chart-topping single. The song talks about accidentally falling in love and was the first tune that featured the words 'number one' in the title to get to the number one spot! Later newspapers reported that Tinchy and the band had fallen out over who wrote the song, but both N-Dubz and the rapper deny this.

" I don't wanna big this up too much, but Tinchy Stryder and N-Dubz on a track, it's gonna be a hit! "

Tinchy Stryder

Artist — The Young Soul Rebels
Song — I Got Soul

In 2009, the band teamed up with a who's who of the UK pop scene to record a single for the War Child charity. Featuring the likes of the Noisettes, Chipmunk and Pixie Lott, the song was a re-working of the Killers' track 'All These Things That I've Done'.

Artist — Mr Hudson
Song — Playing With Fire

N-Dubz's collaboration with Mr Hudson won the band a legion of new fans, a MOBO award and more than 17million views on YouTube! The video is an N-Dubz classic, pitting a clued-up Tulisa against the unfaithful boys.

" The first time we heard Mr Hudson, we knew he was a serious man. We called him up and we wrote bad boy tune together. It took about half an hour! "
Dappy

Artist — Gary Barlow
Song — No One Knows

During the recording of their second album, 'Against All Odds', the band teamed up with Take That main man Gary Barlow to work on a new tune. Little did Tulisa know that she would be working with Gary again as a judge on *The X Factor*.

" Legend. We're big Take That fans and couldn't believe our luck that Gary agreed to do this. "
Fazer

Artist — Bodyrox
Song — We Dance On

N-Dubz and DJ duo Bodyrox got together to work on this pop banger. The catchy song reached number six in the UK charts and was picked to be the theme tune for the film *StreetDance*. It's also one of the most popular, and certainly the cutest, videos of N-Dubz's career, featuring little kids playing the band when they were children!

TUNE!

N-Dubz sound is all their own, but to keep things fresh and creative the band listen to a heady mix of musical styles. So who are the artists that have excited Dappy, Fazer and Tulisa over the years? Their hit list is diverse, unexpected, and super-lyrical! Prepare to be inspired...

HIT LIST

Mungo Jerry
A rock band that was massive in the 1970s. Both Tulisa and Dappy's dads played in it.

Eminem
International rapper with banging rhymes and a flow that's all his own.

Sting
The don. Duku yourself!

Drake
A cool Canadian rapper – check him out!

Chipmunk
Friend and co-collaborator with N-Dubz.

Wu-Tang Clan
New York hip-hop group and Fazer's big inspiration.

George Michael
Amazing singer song-writer who has stood the test of time.

Papoose
Fierce American rapper.

Taskforce
Totally heavy London hip-hop outfit.

Boyz II Men
Tulia's favourite R&B group when she was young.

Phil Collins
Songwriter, drummer, producer and awesome talent. Respect!

Nas
Possibly the most important person in hip-hop.

Tupac
Poet, rapper and actor who died too young.

> "In our spare time me and Fazer will put on Magic FM; other people might class that as a bit, you know, but we don't respond to that. We listen to George Michael, Phil Collins, Duran Duran, who else? Everyone, and that's where you will hear the vocal arrangements and then you go back to your little music and you make something big. It's very helpful, trust me, you need to listen to different music."
>
> Dappy

INSPIRING IPOD

Who's guaranteed to rock your world every time you plug in your headphones? Make a list of your favourite artists here.

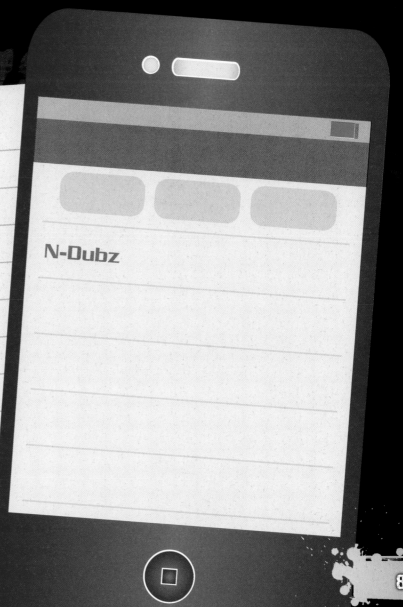

N-Dubz

UNCLE B

As well as being Dappy's dad and Tulisa's uncle, Byron was the band's unofficial manager and producer right from the start. Uncle B used his experience playing bass in Mungo Jerry to show the guys how to find and develop their own musical sound. From about twelve years old, Dappy, Fazer and Tulisa would head to B's recording studio in Dollis Hill to make up chord sequences and lay down new melodies.

Uncle B gave the guys inspiration, motivation and dedication by the bucketful. No matter how far away success seemed, he taught the kids to never, ever give up. Whatever needed to be done to help N-Dubz hit the big time, Uncle B took care of it. He inspired the band's philosophy to always stay true to yourself, to have the courage and pride to be an individual.

Tragically Byron died in 2007, just as N-Dubz were making their first album. From that moment on Dappy, Tulisa and Fazer promised to work even harder to get to the top, in honour of the great man's memory. They dedicated that album to 'Uncle B', then watched as it went platinum.

"Uncle B was everything to us. There would be no N-Dubz without him."
Tulisa

Although he passed away before the N-Dubz became household names, Uncle B did get to see the crew perform their breakthrough song 'I Swear' in an auditorium packed with new fans.

"I looked over at B at the side of the stage and I could see in his face how happy he was. We were living his dream as well as ours. That was one of best moments of my life — when we got off the stage, I'd never seen anything like the look on his face before. He was so happy and telling us we were stars and gonna be famous."
Fazer

Thank you Uncle B, for everything.

> "He knew N-Dubz were a very unique thing from the moment we first got together. He just knew, and that's why he had such belief in us and refused to let negative people around us and our music."
>
> Dappy

TRIV TIME

You've enjoyed the tunes, learnt the rhymes and watched N-Dubz on stage and screen. Are you ready now to take the ultimate trivia quiz? Take the test, check your answers, then clock where you rank on the scoreboard opposite. No cheating!

1. Which North London suburb do the members of N-Dubz hail from?

2. All three members of N-Dubz have acted in a high-profile Channel 4 television show. What is the show called?

3. The band started their career using the name the Likkle Rinsers Crew. They changed their ID once more before settling on N-Dubz. What was the other name that Dappy, Fazer and Tulisa were briefly known by?

4. In 2009, the band nearly missed the chance to perform at Radio 1's Big Weekend as Tulisa was suddenly taken ill. She was eventually given a clean bill of health by doctors and made the gig, but what did the newspapers report that Tulisa had come down with?

5. Which song from the album 'Against All Odds' did R&B artist Mr Hudson contribute to?

6. Dappy has appeared three times on which BBC2 music-based comedy show?

7. The band joined up with a host of stars including Chipmunk, Pixie Lott and Tinchy Stryder to record a song for the War Child charity. What did the super-group call themselves?

8. What is Fazer's real name?

9. After agreeing to stop arguing with Dappy, Tulisa had a word tattooed on her neck to remind her to keep to her side of the deal. What word did she have inked on?

10. Which of the following artists have the band not worked with – Gary Barlow, the Noisettes or Phil Collins?

11. Fazer and Dappy first met when they were just nine years old. Where did they meet?

12. What was the name of the track the band wrote in remembrance of Dappy's father, Uncle B?

....

13. The band have won several important music industry awards. In 2010 they were presented with their fourth MOBO. What category did they win?

....

14. Which N-Dubz single reached the highest position in the Official UK Singles Chart?

....

15. Dappy's real name is Dino Contostavlos, but what is Dino short for?

....

HOW DID YOU DO?

0-5
You haven't earned enough correct answers to call yourself the band's number-one fan yet but don't despair, you already have all the information you need to make it – inside this book! Flick through the pages and try this quiz again – we guarantee you'll do better.

6-10
Nana nana niiiii! Not bad... you've made a decent start in your quest for N-Dubz knowledge, but don't stop yet, there's still a way to go. Keep following the crew and you'll soon get there!

11-15
Duku yourself! What you don't know about the band isn't worth knowing. Your head is so full of N-Dubz facts you could probably teach Dappy, Tulisa and Fazer a thing or two!

A lot has changed for us during the years that we've been together. We've gone from the streets of inner city London to the top of the charts, signing record deals in America and performing all around the world.

N-Dubz are living proof that with talent, hard work and belief everyone can achieve their dreams. The odds were stacked against us and we made it, so there's nothing to stop you from doing the same thing.

Sometimes, when we're shooting a video in an amazing location, are about to walk out on stage or are on our way to an awards show, the three of us will look at each other and smile – we can't believe it. For three street kids from Camden Town, we've done all right! But we couldn't have achieved any of the things we have without you, our true fans.

We are N-Dubz and so are you. Duku yourself!

Dappy, Fazer and Tulisa x

ANSWERS

Pages 18-19
Say It Like It Is!

1. Fazer
2. Dappy
3. Tulisa
4. Dappy
5. Not Dubz
6. Fazer
7. Tulisa
8. Fazer
9. Tulisa
10. Dappy
11. Not Dubz
12. Dappy
13. Fazer
14. Tulisa
15. Dappy

Pages 34-35
Videos In The Mix

1. b
2. d
3. e
4. a
5. f
6. c

Pages 44-45
Rhyme Time

1. I Swear
2. Strong Again
3. Love For My Slum
4. Na Na
5. Playing With Fire
6. No One Knows
7. Scream My Name
8. Best Behaviour
9. Girls
10. Papa Can You Hear Me?

Page 46 – NW1 Wordsearch

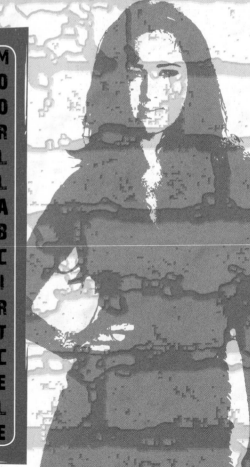

```
D H K K I L O S F X T M
J D R E W O T T B B T E O
R E G E N T S P A R K R O
O T G P W C V A H K R R L
U O V M M E J N E P A L L
N A Z E I Z W C D S M O A
D D M N K S L R J M N L B
H S I N O P A A A X E L C
O E T X K D S S X V D R I
U G Y L K O W N E D F A R
S J F V J Q D O O T M B T
E A E R A K C O L L A C C
Q P X V M B V G S D G E E
D U B L I N C A S T L E L
L G H A B R C A E I P L
U E P X Z S Q L B M M E
```

Page 47
Papped!

Pages 56-57
Read All About It

1. Fake
2. Real
3. Real
4. Real
5. Fake
6. Real
7. Real
8. Fake
9. Fake
10. Real
11. Fake
12. Real
13. Real

Pages 72-73
N-Dubz Deets

1. 3
2. Top 20
3. 4
4. 4
5. 1987
6. 2
7. 27
8. Over 200,000
9. 400%
10. 5
11. 4
12. Twice
13. 300,000
14. 6
15. 768,000

Page 74 – Crew Crossword

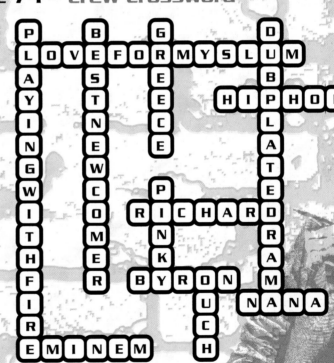

```
P        B       G                D
LOVEFORMYSLUM
A        S       E         H I P H O P
Y        T       E                B
I        N       C                L
N        E  P                     A
G        W  R I C H A R D         T
W        C  I                     E
I        O  N                     R
T        M  K                     A
H        E  B Y R O N             M
F        R  U                     N A N A
I           C
R           H
E M I N E M
```

Pages 86-87 – Triv Time

1. Camden Town
2. Dubplate Drama
3. NW1
4. Swine flu
5. Playing With Fire
6. Never Mind The Buzzcocks
7. The Young Soul Rebels
8. Richard Rawson
9. Dappy
10. Phil Collins – although Dappy's admitted the eighties star is top of his list of dream collaborations
11. At a karate lesson
12. Papa Can You Hear Me?
13. Best song – Playing With Fire
14. I Need You
15. Costas Dinos